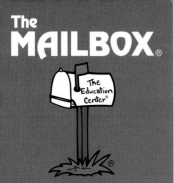

The MAILBOX The Education Center

Trace, Draw, & Crumple

Fine-Motor Skills for Little Learners

Fun activities and practice pages for increasing the following fine-motor skills:

- Strength
- Dexterity
- Control
- Coordination
  And more!

Over 95 ways to develop fine-motor skills!

Editorial Team: Becky S. Andrews, Kimberley Bruck, Diane Badden, Thad H. McLaurin, Sharon Murphy, Kimberly Brugger-Murphy, Kelly Robertson, Karen A. Brudnak, Juli Docimo Blair, Hope Rodgers, Dorothy C. McKinney, Dana Ballou, Janet Boyce, Catherine Broome-Kehm, Ada Goren, Lucia Kemp Henry, Leanne Swinson, Carole Watkins

Production Team: Lori Z. Henry, Pam Crane, Rebecca Saunders, Chris Curry, Sarah Foreman, Theresa Lewis Goode, Greg D. Rieves, Eliseo De Jesus Santos II, Barry Slate, Donna K. Teal, Zane Williard, Tazmen Carlisle, Kathy Coop, Marsha Heim, Lynette Dickerson, Mark Rainey

www.themailbox.com

D1160959

Manufactured in the United States
10 9 8 7 6 5 4 3 2 1

Table of Contents

Why Practice Fine-Motor Skills?

Develop finger, hand, wrist, and arm muscles.

Develop eye-hand control.

Develop eye-muscle control.

Help students
- distinguish letters
- form letters
- track print
and more!

Promote **writing** readiness.

Promote **reading** readiness.

TRACE

Fingertip Writing

Materials
- resealable plastic bags
- permanent marker
- fingerpaint
- clear packing tape

To prepare this center, use the marker to program each resealable bag with a different letter. Then place a dollop of fingerpaint in each bag and reinforce the seals with packing tape. A child visits the center, chooses a bag, and uses his index finger to trace the letter. When he is satisfied with his tracing, he simply rubs his hand over the bag to erase. He continues with the remaining bags in the same manner as time allows.

Colorful Name

Materials
- construction paper —9" x 12" sheet of white
- pencil
- highlighter
- crayon
- glitter glue

Use this project to give a youngster practice tracing her name. In advance, use the pencil to write the child's name on the paper. To begin, a child traces her name with the highlighter. Then she uses a crayon to trace her name again. She completes the project by tracing her name with glitter glue.

Center — Transportation Trace

Little ones rev up their tracing skills when they create these one-of-a-kind vehicles! To make one, a child uses a marker to trace around the block on his paper. Then he traces around the bottom of the cup to create wheels. He uses crayons to add details to his vehicle as desired.

Materials
- drawing paper
- rectangular block
- marker
- small paper cup
- crayons

Individual — Shapely Headband

To make a headband, a youngster chooses a variety of shapes and traces around them on the sentence strip as desired. When she is satisfied with her design, staple the strip so that it fits around her head.

Materials
- sentence strip
- small tagboard shape cutouts
- crayons
- stapler

Nifty Numbers

Materials
- bulletin board paper
- feathers with sturdy tips
- tagboard number cutouts
- shallow container of thinned paint

In advance, place the bulletin board paper on the floor in an open area. Set the feathers, number cutouts, and paint nearby. A child visits the center and places a number cutout on the paper. He dips the tip of a feather in the paint. Then he holds the feather as if it were a pen and traces around the number without pressing down too hard on the tip. He continues tracing different number cutouts in this manner as time allows.

Shiny Shapes

Materials
- construction paper —9" x 12" sheet
- craft foam
- aluminum foil —8" x 11" sheet
- tape
- tagboard shape cutouts
- crayons
- stapler

To prepare a cushioned tracing surface, lightly tape the foil to the craft foam. A youngster places a desired shape cutout on the foil and traces around it with a crayon. She continues tracing around different shapes on the foil until she is satisfied with her project. Then she removes the foil from the craft foam and staples it to the construction paper with assistance.

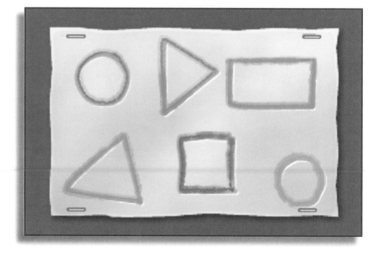

TRACE

Center — Sun, Moon, and Stars

A youngster visits the center, chooses a cutout, and places it on the stardust. She uses her index finger to trace around the cutout and then carefully lifts it to see the resulting shape. After running her hand over the stardust to erase the shape, she traces around additional cutouts as time allows.

Materials
- shallow container of stardust (sand mixed with glitter)
- tagboard cutouts —stars, moons, planets

Center — A Batch of Cookies

To prepare this center, tape the paper to the cookie sheet. A child visits the center, places a cookie cutter on the paper, and uses a pencil to trace around it. She traces around additional cookie cutters as desired. When she is finished tracing, she uses crayons to decorate her tasty treats.

Materials
- cookie sheet
- white paper —cut to fit cookie sheet
- tape
- cookie cutters
- pencil
- crayons

Sweet Strokes

Materials
- sandpaper
  —3½" x 9" strip
- marker
- cinnamon stick
- stapler

These sweet smelling strips are perfect for creating a bulletin board border. To make a strip, a child uses a marker to draw swirly, wavy, or zigzag lines across the sandpaper. Then he traces over the lines several times with the cinnamon stick. Encourage him to sniff the sweet strokes on his strip; then staple it to a bulletin board.

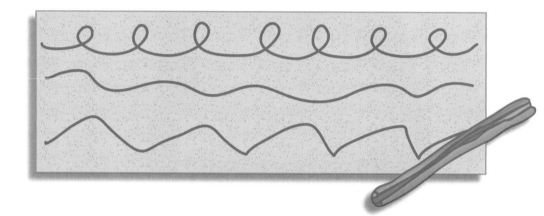

A Dozen Doughnuts

Small Group

Materials
- discarded compact discs (or similar-shaped tagboard cutouts)
- bulletin board paper
- markers

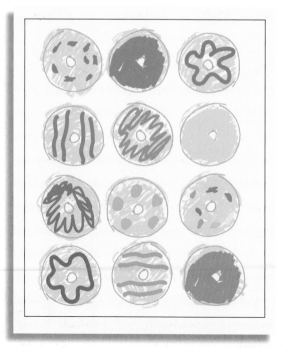

Three students work together to make a dozen doughnuts. To make one doughnut, a youngster uses a marker to trace around the inside and outside of a compact disc on the paper. She traces three more doughnuts in this manner. Then she uses more markers to add desired details, such as sprinkles and icing, to her doughnuts. After each group member has drawn four doughnuts, draw a box around the resulting dozen doughnuts.

TRACE

Interesting Initial

To make a letter creature, a child finds the letter cutout that matches his first initial. He uses a crayon to trace around his initial on the paper. Then he adds details, such as facial features, arms, and legs.

Materials
- construction paper —9" x 12" sheet
- tagboard letter cutouts
- crayons

Center

Around the Block

Invite your class to create a scene of skyscrapers! To prepare, lay the bulletin board paper on the floor in an open area and place the blocks, crayons, and marker nearby. A youngster uses the marker to trace around blocks on the paper to create a tall building. When he is satisfied with his building, he uses the crayons to add desired details. After each child has had a chance to create a skyscraper, post the resulting skyline for everyone to see.

Materials
- bulletin board paper
- a variety of blocks
- marker
- crayons

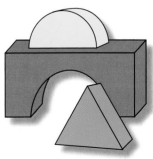

A Huge Honeycomb

Materials
- yellow bee cutouts (patterns on page 12)
- bulletin board paper
- hexagonal blocks
- crayons
- glue

Youngsters trace around hexagons to make a honeycomb at this center! To prepare, lay the bulletin board paper in an open area and set the remaining materials nearby. Each child visits the center and traces around a predetermined number of adjoining hexagons on the paper. When he is finished tracing, he glues a bee cutout in an empty honeycomb cell.

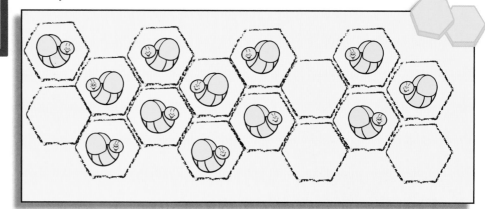

Washing the Car

Materials
- laminated car cutout (pattern on page 13)
- construction paper —9" x 12" sheets
- sponge
- scissors
- clothespin
- shallow tub of water

Invite little ones to wash a car at this center! To prepare, cut the sponge into small squares and clip one square with the clothespin. A youngster visits the center and places the car cutout in the center of the paper. Holding the clothespin, she dips the sponge into the water. She "washes" the car by tracing around the outline of the car with the wet sponge, redipping the sponge as needed. When she is finished, she removes the cutout to see the resulting water outline left on the paper. Then she clips the clothespin to a dry sponge for the next student.

TRACE

Individual

Spring Flowers

To make flowers, a youngster traces around the flower cutout on his paper several times. Then he traces one end of the glue stick (with the cap on) in the center of each flower. He colors his flowers and adds stems and leaves to complete his project.

Materials
- tagboard flower cutout
- drawing paper
- crayons
- glue stick

Individual

Bunny Trail

To help the bunny find the carrots, a youngster traces the path on the reproducible with a thin line of glue. Then he presses the yarn on the glue. After the glue dries, trim any excess yarn.

Materials
- copy of page 14
- glue bottle
- yarn
  —34" length
- scissors

Wavy Water

Materials
- construction paper
  —9" x 12" sheet of white
- tagboard
  —3" x 12" rectangle
- scissors
- crayons

In advance, cut along the width of the tagboard to create a wavy edge. To make a series of waves, a child places the prepared tagboard near the top of her paper and traces along the wavy edge with a blue crayon. She moves the tagboard down and traces it again. She continues in this manner until she has worked her way down the page. Then she draws plants and underwater creatures to create a colorful underwater scene.

Check out the
fine-motor reproducibles
on pages 15–27.

Bee Patterns
Use with "A Huge Honeycomb" on page 10.

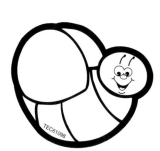

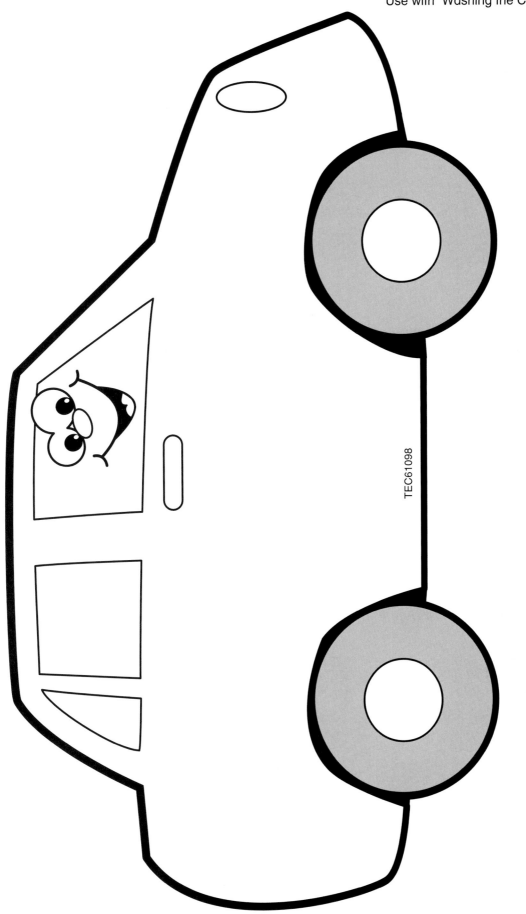

TEC61098

Bunny Trail

START

©The Mailbox® • *Trace, Draw, & Crumple* • TEC61098

14 **Note to the teacher:** Use with "Bunny Trail" on page 11.

Name _____

Snail Trails

Trace.

Falling Raindrops

Trace.

Name

Under the Sea

Trace.

Goal!

 Trace.

Name

It's Party Time!

Trace.

Name _____

Having a Ball

Trace.

Name

Fantastic Flying

Trace.

Off to School!

Trace.

Preschool Express

High in the Sky

Trace.

A Perfect Picnic

Trace.

This way!

Almost there!

Name _____

Happy Hamster

Trace.

Name

Leo the Lion

Trace.

26

Name _____

A Good Flight

Trace.

Bear Air

©The Mailbox® • *Trace, Draw, & Crumple* • TEC61098

27

DRAW & COLOR

Squiggle Art

Materials
- drawing paper
- black marker
- crayons

To create a picture, a youngster uses the marker to draw a closed squiggly design on his paper. Then he uses the crayons to color the spaces between the lines.

Canvas Creation

Materials
- construction paper —9" x 12" sheet of white
- latch hook canvas
- tape
- crayons

To prepare, tape the latch hook canvas to a tabletop and lightly tape the paper over the canvas.

A youngster uses crayons of various colors to color the entire paper. If desired, mount the completed project on a slightly larger sheet of black paper.

Individual

To make a picture, a youngster attaches a predetermined number of self-adhesive dots to his paper as desired. Then he uses the marker to connect the dots.

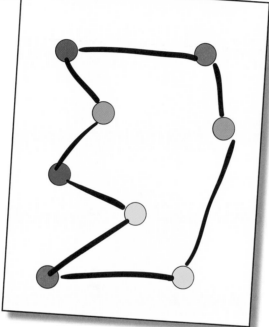

Materials
- self-adhesive dots
- drawing paper
- marker

Individual

Picture-Perfect Puzzle

To prepare a puzzle, place the craft sticks side by side and tape them securely together. Turn the connected sticks over so that the tape is on the back. Then have a child use the markers to draw a picture on the sticks. When she is satisfied with her work, she removes the tape from the back of the sticks (with assistance) and mixes them up. Then she recreates her picture by placing the sticks in the appropriate order. For added fun, challenge youngsters to put together their classmates' puzzles.

Materials
- 8 craft sticks
- masking tape
- markers

Terrific Tree

Materials
- construction paper —6" squares of tan
- large tree cutout
- unwrapped brown crayons
- leaf cutouts

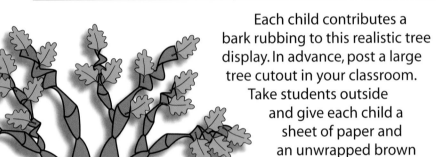

Each child contributes a bark rubbing to this realistic tree display. In advance, post a large tree cutout in your classroom. Take students outside and give each child a sheet of paper and an unwrapped brown crayon. Have her hold the paper against the bark of a tree and rub the side of the crayon over the paper (with assistance if needed). When she is finished, she glues the completed bark to the trunk of the tree cutout. Attach leaf cutouts or student-made leaf rubbings to the branches to complete the display.

Magic Jack-o'-Lantern

Press hard when coloring this project, and a jack-o'-lantern magically appears! To begin, a youngster folds the paper in half as if making a card. Next, he unfolds the paper and presses hard with the side of the crayon to color the left side of the paper. Then he refolds the paper and presses hard with the dull pencil to draw a jack-o'-lantern on the front of the folded paper. When he unfolds the paper again, the jack-o'-lantern has magically appeared inside!

Materials
- construction paper —9" x 12" sheet of orange
- unwrapped black crayon
- dull pencil

DRAW & COLOR

Individual   Striped Zebra

To create a zany zebra, a child uses the crayon to draw stripes on the zebra shape. As he draws, encourage him to vary the appearance of the lines. For example, he may draw thick, thin, wavy, or straight lines, or he may color with heavy or light strokes. If desired, cut out the zebra and mount it to a 9" x 12" sheet of black paper.

Materials
- copy of page 39
- black crayon

Individual   Colorful Drawing

To make one, a child chooses three to four crayons and bundles them together in her fist. Then she draws zigzags, loops, and squiggles on her paper as desired. Encourage her to add more color to her drawing by replacing the crayons in her bundle with crayons of different colors.

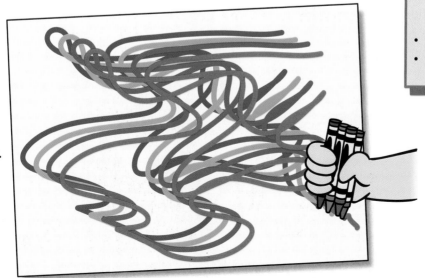

Materials
- standard-size crayons
- drawing paper

Nifty Name

Materials
- construction paper
  —12" x 18" sheet of white
- tagboard letter stencils
- tape
- unwrapped crayon

To prepare, help a child spell his name with the letter stencils. Attach small pieces of rolled tape to the backs of the stencils and stick them to a tabletop. Lay the paper over the stencils and lightly tape it in place. The child rubs the side of a crayon over the paper using different strokes (side to side and top to bottom). He continues in this manner until all the letters in his name have been revealed.

Polka-Dot Puppy

Materials
- puppy cutout
  (pattern on page 40)
- crayons

To make a puppy, a student uses a crayon to draw spots on the cutout as desired. Then she colors the facial features to complete the project.

DRAW & COLOR

Whole Group

Musical Coloring

Use music to help little ones distinguish between coloring with heavy and light strokes. To begin, play a selection of fast music and then a selection of slow music. Lead a discussion comparing the two types of music. Give each youngster a sheet of paper and crayons. Play a selection of fast or slow music and have each child color on his paper in a manner that corresponds with the sounds he hears. For example, if the music is slow, he colors with soft, gentle strokes. If the music is fast, he colors with hard, fast strokes. For an interesting effect, switch between playing slow and fast music as each youngster experiments with his strokes.

Materials
- recordings of fast and slow music
- drawing paper
- crayons

Individual

Personalized Pajamas

To make personalized pajamas, a child draws desired decorations on her pajama top and bottom cutouts. Then she draws details on the face so it resembles her own. When she is satisfied with her work, she glues the pajama top and bottom together as shown (with assistance). Then she draws her hair to complete the project.

Materials
- pajama cutouts (patterns on page 41 and 42)
- crayons
- glue

Colorful Filter

Materials
- coffee filter
- washable markers
- spray bottle of water

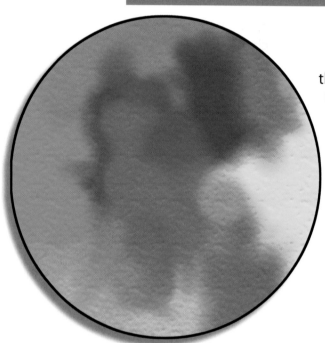

To begin, a child flattens the coffee filter on a covered tabletop and uses the markers to color the filter as desired. Then she gently sprays the filter with water to blend the colors. When the coffee filter is dry, use the colorful creation as part of a flower or as a backing for the child's photo.

On the Road!

Materials
- bulletin board paper
- unwrapped black crayons
- crayons of other colors
- toy car

Get your youngsters on the road to better fine-motor skills with this center activity. First, a child makes a straight road by drawing a thick line on the paper with the side of an unwrapped black crayon. Then he makes a curvy road by turning the crayon while drawing. When he is satisfied with his two roads, he uses the other crayons to add details such as bushes and

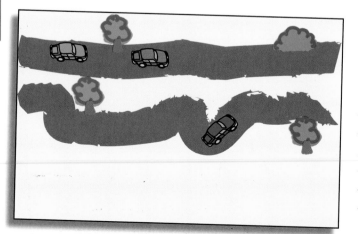

trees beside his roads. Then he "drives" a toy car along the resulting roadways. Encourage each center visitor to add additional roads to the project. When the paper has plenty of roads, replace it with a clean sheet for the remaining center visitors. Vroom, vroom!

DRAW & COLOR

Rub a Rainbow

To make a rainbow, a youngster uses chalk to color thick lines on the half circle. She gently rubs the chalk to blend the colors. When the desired effect is achieved, lightly spray her rainbow with hairspray to prevent the chalk from rubbing off the paper. When the hairspray is dry, the child glues her rainbow onto the blue paper and adds desired details.

Materials
- construction paper
  —8" half circle of white
  —9" x 12" sheet of light blue
- chalk
- aerosol hairspray
  (for teacher use only)
- glue
- crayons

Creative Caterpillar

Individual

To make a caterpillar, a child draws three circles on the paper as shown. Then he adds antennae, eyes, a mouth, and legs. For an added touch, he draws details such as stripes or polka dots on the caterpillar's body.

Materials
- drawing paper
- colored pencils

35

Chalk Mural

Materials
- bulletin board paper
- masking tape
- colored chalk

To create a texture-rich mural, tape the paper to an open area of concrete outside. Students use the tips and sides of the chalk pieces to draw colorful designs or pictures on the paper.

Stained Glass Picture

Materials
- clear plastic wrap
- tape
- permanent markers

To begin, tape a piece of plastic wrap to a child's work area. The youngster draws a picture on the plastic wrap using the permanent markers. When he is satisfied with his picture, tape it to a classroom window for a stained glass effect.

DRAW & COLOR

Individual
Textured Tape

To make a design, a youngster tears various lengths of masking tape and arranges them on a sheet of paper as desired, overlapping the tape pieces to create dimension. Then he uses the clear tape to lightly tape the other sheet on top of the design and rubs the sides of different-colored crayons over the paper until the design is revealed.

Materials
- white paper —2 sheets
- masking tape
- unwrapped crayons
- clear tape

Individual
Wonderful Watermelon

To make a watermelon slice, a child colors the border of the paper plate green so it resembles a rind. He colors the rest of the plate red so it resembles the flesh. Then he draws black seeds to complete his tasty creation.

Materials
- half of a 10" paper plate
- crayons

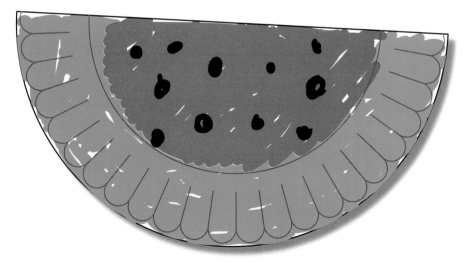

Fish in the Sea

Materials
- colorful fish cutouts (pattern on page 43)
- copy paper
- bubble wrap
- tape
- unwrapped blue crayon
- green crayon

In advance, tape the bubble wrap to a tabletop. To create an underwater scene, a youngster places the paper on top of the bubble wrap and rubs the side of the blue crayon on the paper. Then he glues each fish cutout to his paper as desired. To complete the scene, he uses a green crayon to add seaweed.

Flashy Fish

Materials
- aluminum foil
- black permanent marker
- bright-colored crayons

In advance, use the marker to draw a simple fish shape on a piece of foil. To make a flashy fish, a child uses the crayons to color the fish, varying her strokes so that some are long and sweeping, some are circular, and others are wavy.

Check out the fine-motor reproducibles on pages 44–53.

38

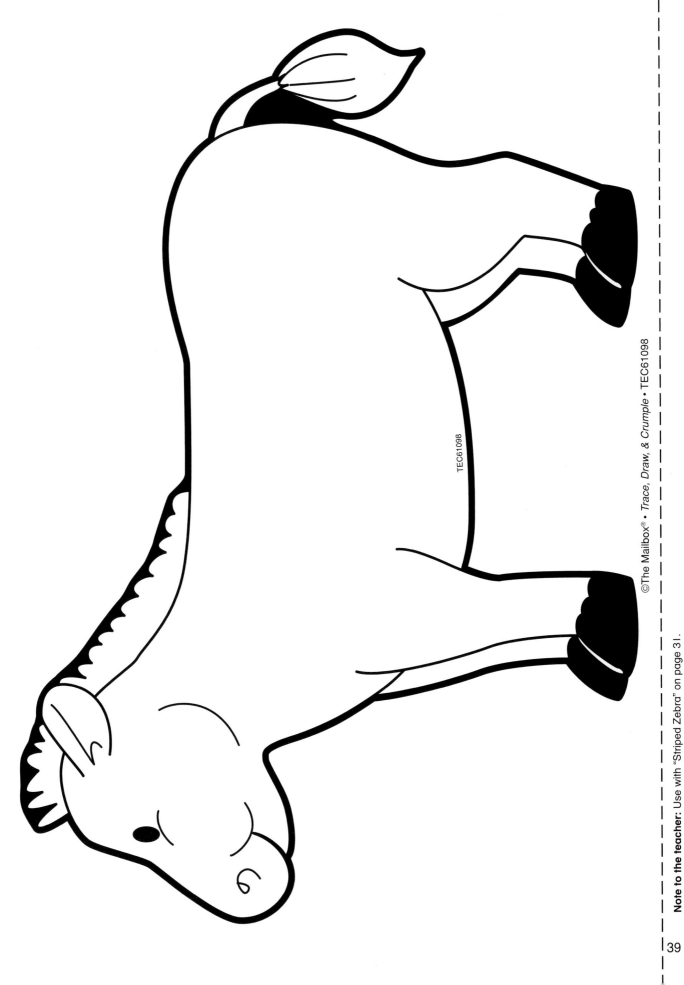

Note to the teacher: Use with "Striped Zebra" on page 31.

Puppy Pattern
Use with "Polka-Dot Puppy" on page 32.

TEC61098

TEC61098

Pajama Bottom Pattern

Use with "Personalized Pajamas" on page 33.

Glue here.

TEC61098

Name

Hats for Hippo

Color.

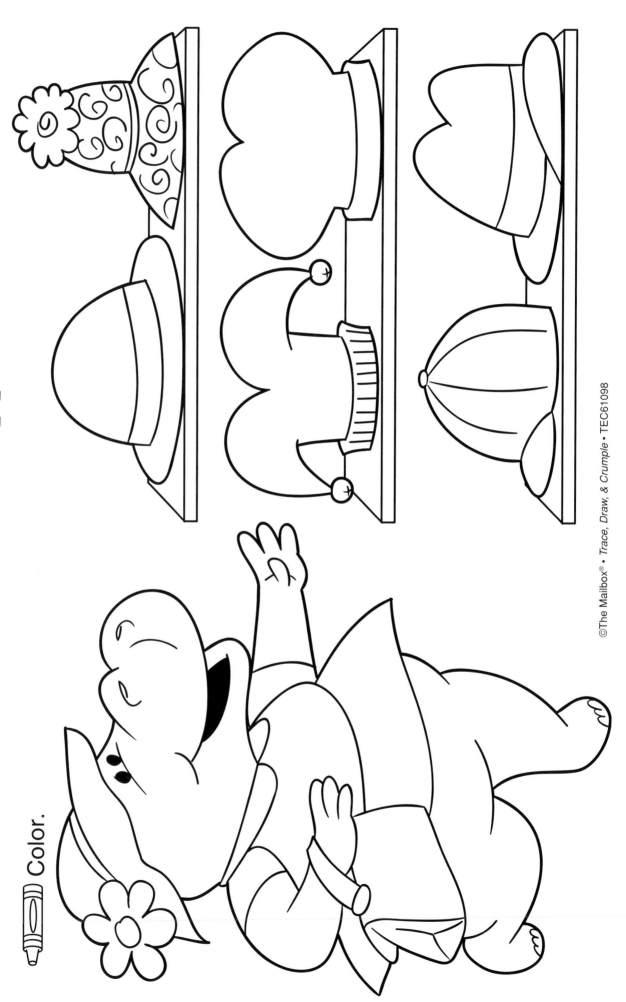

Bunches of Bubbles

 Draw ⬭o .

Up, Up, and Away

 Draw 🎈.

Name

Cool Cones

Draw.

Name

Splish, Splash!

Draw  .

Name _____

Proud Peacock

Draw ⬮.

49

Outside Fun

Finish the picture.

Funny Face

Finish the monkey.

Pretty Pig

Finish the pig.

Cuddly Friend

Finish the teddy bear.

CRUMPLE & SQUEEZE

Gumballs Galore!

Materials
- copy of page 72
- crayons
- tissue paper squares
- glue stick

A youngster colors the base of the gumball machine as desired. To make a gumball, he tightly crumples a tissue paper square and glues it on his gumball machine. He continues to work until his machine contains a colorful assortment of tissue paper gumballs. If desired, cut out the gumball machines and display them with the title "Gumballs Galore!"

Fall Foliage

Materials
- light brown bulletin board paper
- thick black marker
- tape
- paper towels
- red, yellow, and orange diluted food coloring
- eyedroppers
- glue

In advance, use the marker to draw a large tree shape on the bulletin board paper as shown. Then attach the paper to a table. Give each youngster a paper towel; then encourage her to use the eyedroppers to gently squeeze diluted food coloring on the paper towel. After the paper towels are dry, place them at the prepared table along with the glue.

To use the center, a youngster tears small pieces from the prepared paper towels, and then glues the pieces to the tree. Students continue until the tree is full of colorful leaves.

Individual   Pop! Pop! Pop!

A child glues the popcorn box cutout to the red paper. She crumples one of the copy paper scraps into a ball that resembles a piece of popcorn. She dips the popcorn into the glue and then presses it above the popcorn box. She continues in the same way with other scraps of copy paper, adding popcorn above and around the box.

Materials
- yellow popcorn box cutout (pattern on page 73)
- construction paper —9" x 12" sheet of red
- copy paper scraps
- shallow container of glue

Individual   Spooky Spider

To make a spider body, a student crumples the black paper into a tight ball. Then, on the other piece of paper, she draws a dragline from which her spooky spider might dangle. As the student looks on, securely tape the wadded paper ball to the end of the dragline. To complete her project, the student glues the hole-punch dots (eyes) to the body and uses a crayon to draw eight spider legs.

Materials
- construction paper —9" square of black —6" x 9" of any bright color
- crayons
- tape
- hole-punch dots
- glue

Fancy Fishbowl

Materials
- fish cutout
  (pattern on page 43)
- blue fishbowl cutout
  (pattern on page 74)
- construction paper
  —scraps of various
    colors
- glue
- crayons
- paintbrush
- hole puncher

A child glues the fish cutout to the bowl; then she uses crayons to draw any desired fishbowl accessories, such as seaweed. She brushes glue over the lower portion of the bowl. To complete the project, she squeezes the hole puncher to produce hole-punch dots from the paper scraps, allowing the dots to fall on the glue.

Lunar Landscape

Materials
- construction paper
  —9" x 12" sheet of black
- 9" waxed paper circle
- glue
- star stickers

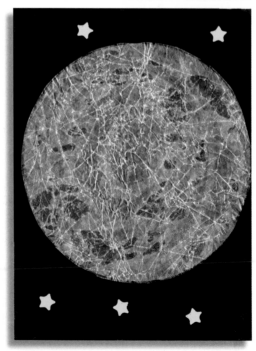

A youngster crumples the waxed paper circle; then he smoothes it out. The result resembles the moon and its bumps and craters. He glues the moon to the construction paper sheet. Then he decorates the space scene with star stickers.

CRUMPLE & SQUEEZE

Small Group
Ring Toss

In advance, trim the bottom from a lunch bag for each child. (Discard the bottoms of the bags or save them for a future craft activity.) Place the plastic hoop on the floor in a traffic-free area of your room. Place a tape line on the floor a few feet away from the plastic hoop. Then gather a small group of youngsters. Each child crumples the sides of his bag to make a ring as shown. Then he stands on the tape line and tosses his ring, attempting to make it land in the hoop.

Materials
- paper lunch bags
- scissors
- plastic hoop
- masking tape

Individual
Marvelous Moon Rocks

To make a moon rock, a child crumples a piece of aluminum foil to create a loose ball. She dabs black paint over the ball in a random fashion. Then she sprinkles the silver and gold glitter over the wet paint and sets the ball aside to dry.

Materials
- aluminum foil
- black tempera paint
- paintbrush
- silver and gold glitter

Falling Snow

Materials
- blue bulletin board paper
- tape
- markers
- tissues
- shallow container of glue

In advance, tape a length of bulletin board paper to a table and draw a simple outdoor scene similar to the one shown. Place the tissues and the container of glue nearby. A child visits the center. She tears a piece of tissue and crumples it into a ball. She dips the ball into glue; then she places it on the paper so that it resembles falling snow. She continues in this manner as time allows.

Doorknob Wreath

Materials
- green wreath cutout (pattern on page 75)
- red bow cutout (pattern on page 75)
- tissue paper squares —red, green
- shallow container of glue
- yarn
- tape

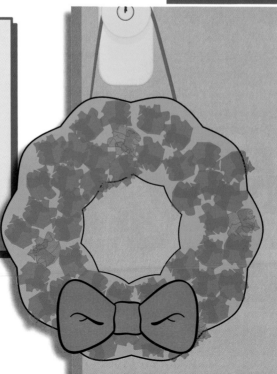

A youngster chooses four red squares. She crumples each one, dips it into glue, and then places it on the wreath to make a holly berry. She continues in the same way with as many green squares as she needs to fill in the spaces around the berries. She glues the red bow cutout to the wreath. Then, when the glue is dry, she tapes a loop of yarn to the back of the wreath (with assistance) to make a hanger.

CRUMPLE & SQUEEZE

Center — Crumpled Cookies

Crumple the brown paper scraps and place them in the bowl. Put the bowl at a center along with the tongs and cookie sheet. A youngster squeezes the tongs to pick up a crumpled piece of paper; then he places the paper on the sheet so that it resembles a ball of cookie dough. He continues in the same way, attempting to place the cookie-dough balls in straight lines just like a real chef!

Materials
- construction paper —scraps of brown
- mixing bowl
- tongs
- cookie sheet

Center — Awesome Ornaments

Cut a large Christmas tree shape from green bulletin board paper and attach a brown trunk cutout. Laminate the tree and then tape it to a table. Place several colors of play dough at the table. A child squishes and squeezes a piece of play dough into a ball; then she places the resulting ornament on the tree. She continues in the same way, decorating the tree with a variety of lovely play dough ornaments.

Materials
- bulletin board paper —green, brown
- scissors
- tape
- play dough

Mr. Mouth

Materials
- utility knife (teacher use only)
- tennis ball
- permanent marker
- milk-jug lids

To prepare, use the utility knife to cut a slit in a tennis ball so that it resembles a mouth as shown. Draw eyes and a nose on the ball. Place the ball at a center along with several milk-jug lids. A child squeezes the ball, causing the mouth to open. Then she feeds milk-jug lids to this cute character.

Baggy Beanbags

Materials
- personalized resealable plastic bag
- scrap paper
- 3 jingle bells
- clear packing tape

Jayden

To make a beanbag, a child crumples pieces of scrap paper and then stuffs the pieces into his resealable plastic bag. If desired, invite the child to decorate his bag with stickers. Before sealing the bag with packing tape, drop in the jingle bells. Encourage youngsters to use the resulting bags for simple games and toss-and-catch activities.

CRUMPLE & SQUEEZE

Individual — Lunch Bag Masterpiece

Have the youngster crumple and then straighten a lunch bag several times. When the bag is soft and wrinkled, cut it open to make a panel that measures approximately 8" x 10". Next, have the youngster glue the panel to the sheet of construction paper. Then direct her to crumple and glue tissue paper scraps to the project as desired.

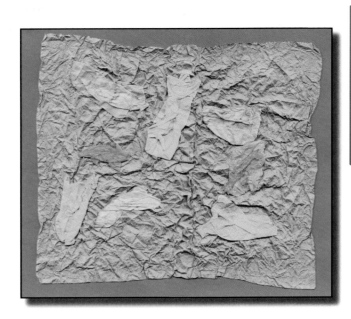

Materials
- construction paper —9" x 12" sheet
- paper lunch bag
- scissors
- tissue paper scraps
- glue

Center — Drip, Drop!

Use the food coloring to tint each cup of water a different color. Place the cups at a center along with the paper and eyedroppers. A child visits the center and gently squeezes the eyedropper to drip a variety of colorful drops on the white paper. If desired, mount the resulting artwork on a larger, colorful sheet of construction paper.

Materials
- construction paper —9" x 12" sheets of white
- food coloring
- cups of water
- eyedroppers

Woolly Lamb

Materials
- lamb cutout
  (pattern on page 76)
- construction paper
  —12" green strip
  —9" x 12" sheet
- glue stick
- tissue paper
  —scraps of white
- scissors
- shallow container of glue

A child fringe-cuts the green strip of paper so that it resembles grass and glues the grass to the bottom of the construction paper sheet. She glues the lamb cutout above the grass. Next, she crumples a piece of tissue paper and dips it into the container of glue. Then she presses it onto the lamb. She continues in the same way until the lamb is covered with tissue paper wool.

Rainbow Toss

Materials
- construction paper
  —scraps of red, orange, yellow, green, blue, purple

Give each child a construction paper scrap. Have little ones crumple their construction paper and then conceal it in their hands. Next, lead students in reciting the chant shown. During the fourth line of the chant, have little ones open their hands and toss the paper into the air to create a rainbow. To play again, direct each child to pick up a scrap of a different color. Then lead them in the chant again.

Red, orange, yellow, green,
Lots of colors to be seen!
There's some blue and purple too,
A rainbow just for me and you!

CRUMPLE & SQUEEZE

Center

Bunny Tails

Place the bunny cutouts at a center along with the cotton balls and the clothespin. A youngster squeezes the clothespin to pick up a cotton ball; then he squeezes it again to release the cotton ball over a bunny cutout, giving the bunny an adorable fluffy tail. He repeats the process until each bunny has a tail.

Materials
- bunny cutouts (pattern on page 73)
- cotton balls
- clothespin

Small Group

The Name Game

Gather a small group of youngsters and have them sit in a circle. Secretly write one of the youngsters' names on the sheet of copy paper. Crumple the paper and then give it to a student. Have the child roll the die and identify the number. Then encourage students to pass the paper to their left a corresponding number of times. The youngster holding the paper smoothes it out and checks to see whether the name is her own. If it isn't, the youngster crumples the paper again and play continues in the same fashion. If the paper does have her name on it, she gets to keep the paper. A new name is then written on another piece of paper for another round of The Name Game!

Materials
- copy paper
- marker
- large die

Blooming Flowers

Materials
- colorful scarves

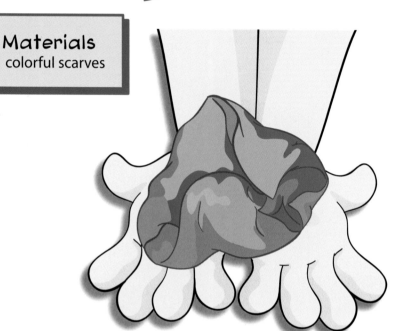

Have each child crumple a scarf and hold it tightly in her hands, concealing it as much as possible. Next, lead little ones in reciting the poem below. After the last line is read, have each youngster slowly open her hands to reveal a lovely, colorful blossom. Encourage each student to name the color of her scarf. Then have youngsters switch scarves and repeat the activity.

The flowers are just little buds.
They're closed up tight, you see.
But soon the flowers all will bloom.
What colors will they be?

April Showers Art

Materials
- construction paper
  —9" x 12" sheet of white
- plastic spray bottle
- water
- blue tempera paint
- newspaper
- crayons

To prepare, partially fill a spray bottle with water. Drizzle blue tempera paint into the water; then secure the cap. Shake the spray bottle to mix the water and paint. A youngster uses the crayons to draw a picture on the construction paper. She takes her picture outside and places it on a layer of old newspapers; then she squeezes the spray bottle to mist tinted water over the picture. Now she has a rain-splattered masterpiece!

CRUMPLE & SQUEEZE

Individual

Splendid Spring Tree

A youngster colors the tree trunk and branches. Then he crumples a square of tissue paper, dips it in the glue, and presses it on the tree. He continues in the same way to make a lovely blossom-filled tree!

Materials
- copy of page 77
- crayons
- tissue paper squares —yellow, pink
- shallow container of glue

Whole Group

Toss and Catch

Have each child crumple a piece of cellophane and conceal it in one hand. Then play the music and encourage youngsters to dance. After a suitable amount of time has elapsed, stop the music and say, "Toss and catch!" Encourage youngsters to toss and then catch their cellophane squares. Once tossed, the cellophane floats slowly to the floor, making it easy to catch. Have students re-crumple the cellophane squares; then continue in the same way for another round of play.

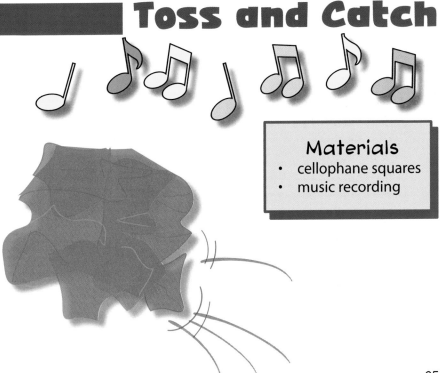

Materials
- cellophane squares
- music recording

Picking Blueberries

Materials
- large green bush cutout
- blue pom-poms
- basket
- clothespin

Place the bush at a center; then scatter the pom-poms on the bush so they resemble blueberries. Set the basket and clothespin near the bush. A youngster squeezes the clothespin to pick up a berry and then squeezes it again to release it into the basket. He continues in the same way until all of the berries have been placed in the basket.

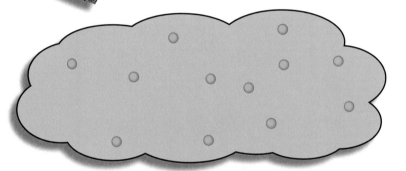

Pretty Petals

Materials
- paper cups
- scissors
- tissue paper of various colors
- plastic clothespins
  —colors to match tissue paper

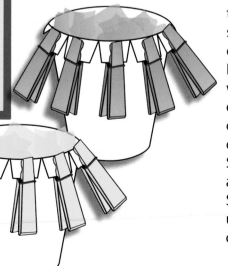

Make one-inch cuts around the edge of each cup. Then bend the resulting tabs outward as shown. Stuff the center of each cup with a piece of tissue paper. Place the cups in a center along with a supply of colorful plastic clothespins. A child identifies the color of the tissue paper; then she chooses a matching clothespin. She squeezes the clothespin and attaches it to one of the tabs. She continues in the same way until all the cups have matching clothespin petals.

CRUMPLE & SQUEEZE

Beautiful Butterfly

Individual

To make a butterfly, a child crumples tissue paper and places it in the plastic bag. She removes the air from the bag and then seals the bag (with assistance). She gathers the middle of the bag. Then she twists a pipe cleaner around the middle, as shown, to form the butterfly's body and antennae.

Materials
- tissue paper scraps
- resealable plastic bag
- pipe cleaner

Happy Plants

Individual

Partially fill a spray bottle with water and set the nozzle on the mist option. A youngster takes the spray bottle outside during outdoor playtime. He squeezes the handle and mists the plants in the play area, including the trees and grass. He gets a fine-motor workout, and the plants get a nice healthy bath!

Materials
- spray bottle
- water

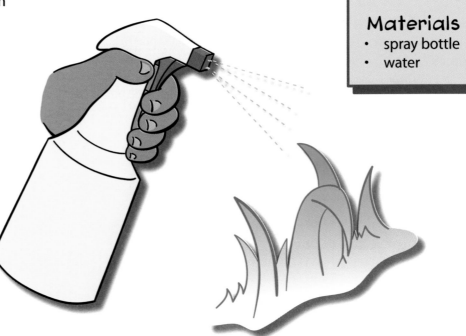

Shaving Cream Squeeze

Materials
- nonmentholated shaving cream
- resealable plastic bag
- scissors
- building block

Place shaving cream in the bag. Work the shaving cream down into one corner of the bag; then snip off the tip of the corner and give the bag to a youngster. The child squeezes the bag as if he were a pastry chef, covering a building block with shaving cream frosting. It looks just like a tasty cake!

Well-Fed Fishy

Materials
- construction paper
  —scraps of various colors
- newspaper pieces
- paper lunch bag
- twist-tie
- tempera paint
- small sponge pieces
- glue

To make a fish, a child crumples several pieces of newspaper and stuffs them into the bag. When his bag is nearly full, he uses a twist-tie (with assistance) to close the opening of his bag and form a tail for his fish as shown. Next, he sponge-paints his fish to his liking. When the paint has dried, he tears two fins and two eyes from paper scraps; then he glues them to his colorful fish.

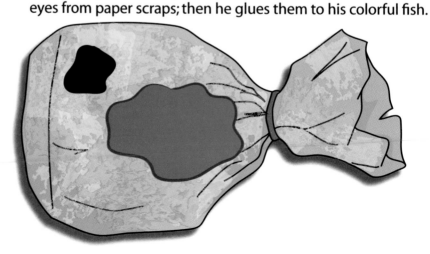

CRUMPLE & SQUEEZE

Whole Group
Slam Dunk

Turn clean-up time into a game of hoops. Place a masking tape line near a wastebasket. After a paper-cutting activity, ask students to pick up paper scraps and crumple them. Then have each child stand on the tape line, in turn, and toss her scrap into the wastebasket. Encourage students to repeat the activity until the scraps have all been placed in the wastebasket.

Materials
- masking tape
- wastebasket
- wastepaper

Individual
Clown Soaker

Draw a simple clown picture on the poster board. Laminate the poster board. Then post it at a child's eye level in your outdoor play area. Partially fill the tub with water and place it nearby. Fill the bottle with water as well and set it near the tub. A child opens the top of the water bottle, aims it toward the clown, and then squeezes the bottle. When the youngster has emptied the bottle, he refills it for the next child using the water in the tub.

Materials
- poster board
- markers
- masking tape
- plastic tub
- water
- pull-top water bottle

Patriotic Play Dough
Center

Materials
- play dough
  —red, white, blue
- silver glitter
- star cookie cutter

Mix silver glitter with the red, blue, and white play dough. Then place the play dough at a center along with the star cookie cutter. A youngster takes a piece of each playdough color and squishes and squeezes the pieces together to make a swirly ball of patriotic play dough. Then she flattens the play dough and uses the cookie cutter to make lovely stars.

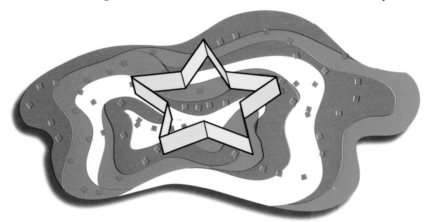

Fireflies!
Individual

Materials
- construction paper
  —9" x 12" sheet of black
- yellow moon cutout
- glue
- aluminum foil squares
- craft glue
- white crayon

A child glues the moon cutout to the paper. Then she crumples the squares of aluminum foil into balls and uses the craft glue to glue them to the paper to make the bodies of the fireflies. When the glue is dry, she uses the white crayon to draw wings on each firefly.

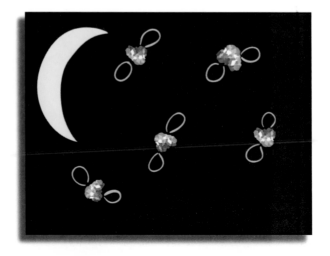

CRUMPLE & SQUEEZE

Small Group

Bucket to Bucket

To set up this game, position the buckets five feet apart. Gather a small group of children and have them stand in a line. The first child in line soaks the sponge in the first bucket, carries it to the second bucket, and squeezes out the water. Then she gives the sponge to the next child in line. Students continue in the same way until all of the water has been transferred to the second bucket.

Materials
- bucket of water
- empty bucket
- sponge

Individual

No Brush Needed

A youngster crumples a sheet of newspaper into a loose ball. He presses the ball in the paint and then proceeds to paint the construction paper as desired, using both sweeping and twisting motions as well as making prints to create a desired effect. He repeats the process with other colors of paint.

Materials
- construction paper —12" x 18" sheet
- newspaper
- shallow containers of tempera paint

Check out the fine-motor reproducibles on pages 78–80.

TEC61098

Note to the teacher: Use with "Gumballs Galore!" on page 54.

Popcorn Box Pattern
Use with "Pop! Pop! Pop!" on page 55.

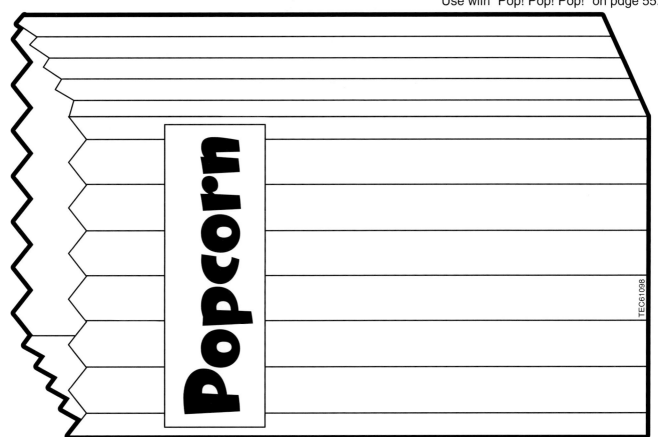

Bunny Pattern
Use with "Bunny Tails" on page 63.

Fishbowl Pattern
Use with "Fancy Fishbowl" on page 56.

TEC61098

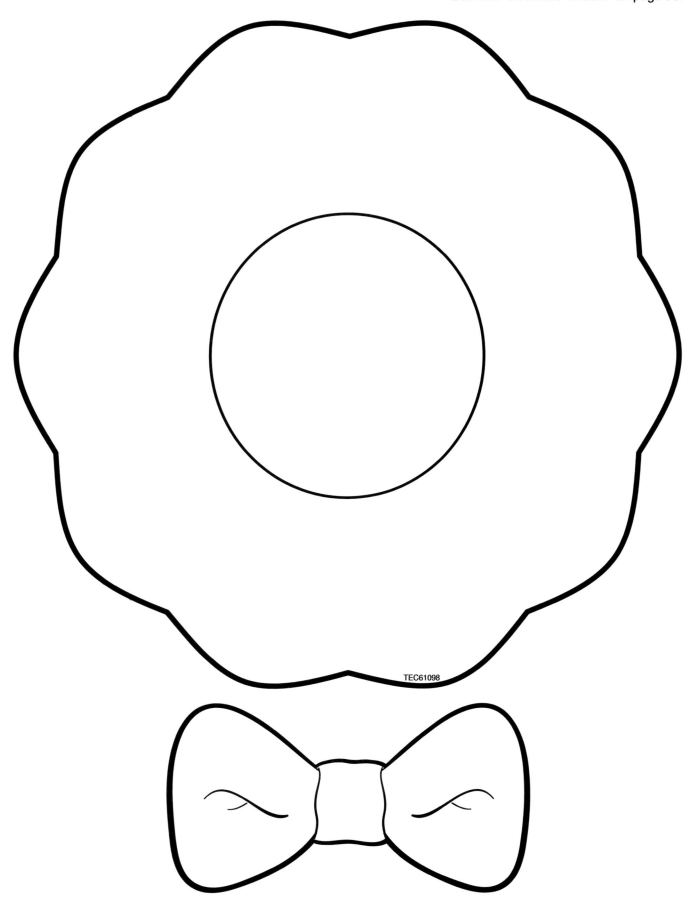

TEC61098

Lamb Pattern
Use with "Woolly Lamb" on page 62.

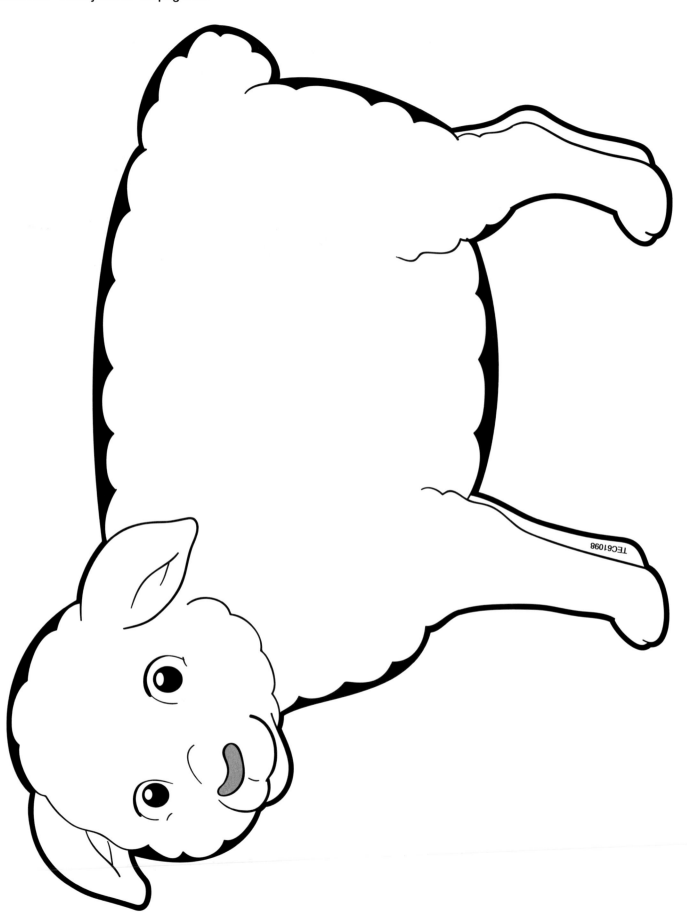

TEC61098

TEC61098

©The Mailbox® • *Trace, Draw, & Crumple* • TEC61098

Apples, Apples, Apples!

Color.

Crumple.

Glue.

Apples Apples Apples

Note to the teacher: Provide small squares of red tissue paper. Have children crumple the squares into small balls and then glue them to the tree so that they resemble apples.

Name _____

Lovely Ladies

Color.

Crumple.

Glue.

Note to the teacher: Provide small squares of black tissue paper. Have children crumple the squares into small balls and then glue them to the bugs to make spots.

Trash Day

 Color.

 Crumple. Glue.

Note to the teacher: Provide small scraps of colored paper. Have children crumple the scraps and then glue them to the garbage truck and can so they resemble trash.